J. B. Lippincott Junior Books
10 East 53rd Street
New York, New York 10022

Library of Congress Cataloging-in-Publication Data
Drescher, Henrik.
   Whose furry nose?

   Summary: Walking through the Australian wilderness, a
young boy encounters many different types of animals.
    1. Zoology—Australia—Juvenile literature.   2. Animals
—Juvenile literature.   [1. Zoology—Australia.
2. Questions and answers]   I. Title.
QL338.D74 1987   599.0994   87–45151
ISBN 0-397-32236-4
ISBN 0-397-32243-7 (lib. bdg.)

WHOSE
FURRY NOSE?

AUSTRALIAN ANIMALS YOU'D LIKE TO MEET
BY HENRIK DRESCHER

J.B. LIPPINCOTT
NEW YORK

Whose leaping legs?

a wallaby's

Whose bright eyes?

spotted cuscuses'

Whose black-and-white stripes?

a numbat's

platypuses'

Whose strong tail?

a climbing kangaroo's

Whose yellow belly?

a yellow belly glider's

Whose furry nose?

a koala's

CLIMBING KANGAROOS

Climbing kangaroos are small tree animals. They have long, furry tails and move from branch to branch by hopping. Climbing kangaroos have strong foreclaws and hindlegs that help them to walk forward and backward in the treetops.

CUSCUSES

Cuscuses live in trees and travel by reaching from one branch to another. Their fur can be many different colors, such as copper red, silver-grey, or black. Cuscuses are just like possums, only their eyes and coats are brighter. They come out at night and use their bright eyes to search for food.

WALLABIES

Wallabies are just like kangaroos, only smaller. They live on the open plains, in the forest, and on rocky slopes and cliffs. Wallabies have pouches to carry their babies in as they hop around on their big back legs looking for grasses to eat.

NUMBATS

Numbats are delicate animals with black-and-white stripes across the lower part of their bodies. They spend most of their time searching for their favorite food—termites. In summer, numbats sunbathe on logs.

KOALAS

Koalas live in trees and like to come out at night. They eat the leaves and buds of eucalyptus trees. Baby koalas ride on their mothers' backs until they are eleven months old.

YELLOW BELLY GLIDERS

Yellow belly gliders have a thin, furred skin between their front and back legs, which helps them to glide in the air from tree to tree. They cut large, V-shaped notches into the bark of eucalyptus and wattle trees to get the sap and gum they eat. They also eat pollen and insects. Yellow belly gliders screech and gurgle during their flights.

PLATYPUSES

The platypus has the body of a mammal but the face of a duck. It lays eggs like a reptile but nurses its young as mammals do. The platypus is covered with waterproof fur and gets all of its food from the water.